This book belongs to

_____

Ninja Life Hacks™

This book is dedicated to my children - Mikey, Kobe, and Jojo.

978-1-951056-65-0 Printed and bound in the USA. NinjaLifeHacks.tv

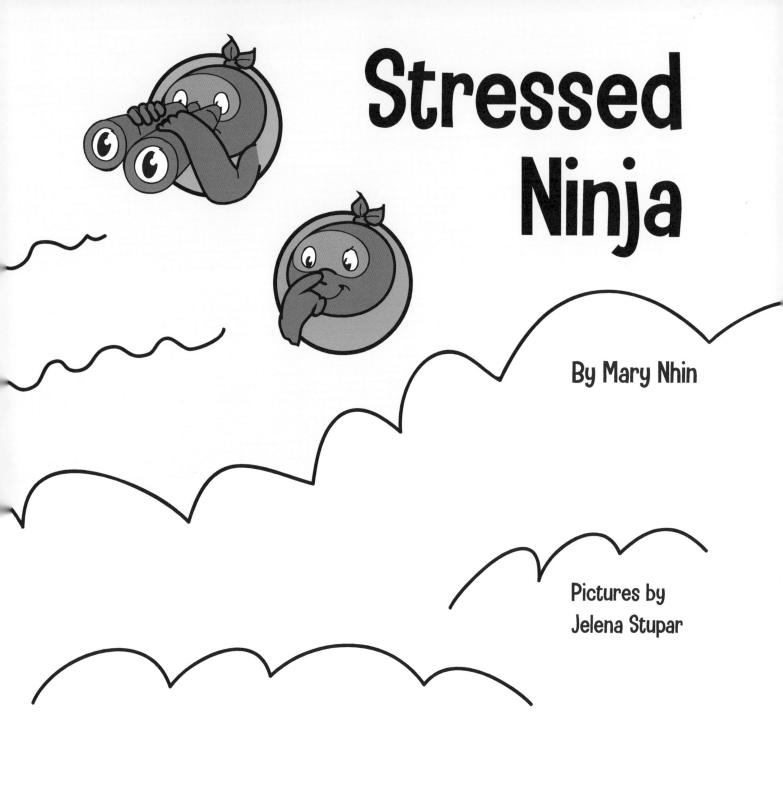

Stressed Ninja

By Mary Nhin

Pictures by
Jelena Stupar

I have mastered the art of relaxation. When stressful events occur, I don't become filled with worry or anxiety.

I've learned how to keep calm under the most stressful situations.

I haven't always understood how to relax and remain stress-free.

In fact, my reactions would cause others to not want to be near me.

I just didn't know how to deal with my stress and the loss of control I felt.

For example, I would feel anxious when starting on a new sports team.

When I learned my family was moving, I cried because of the uncertainty.

If there were a lot of things on my schedule for the week,
I would worry and fret about fitting it all in.

The stress was real in my life. I often developed a rash and fever sores from the stress I felt.

Until one day, Hopeful Ninja introduced me to a very simple but powerful concept.

Do you feel stress sometimes, too? Would you like to find out how I turn my stress into calm?

I like using the 5-4-3-2-1 when I feel stressed.

Look around for 5 things that you can see, and say them out loud.

For example, you could say, *I see the sun. I see the tree. I see the flowers. I see the ants. I see the twig.*

Pay attention to your body and think of 4 things
that you can feel, and say them out loud.

For example, you could say, *I feel my feet on the grass. I feel my hand on the tree. I feel my fingers on the flower. And I feel the twig.*

Listen for 3 sounds. It could be the sound of traffic outside, the sound of birds singing, or the sound of your tummy rumbling. Say the three things out loud.

If you're allowed to, it's okay to move to another spot and sniff something. If you can't smell anything at the moment or you can't move, then name your 2 favorite smells.

Say 1 thing you can taste. It may be the toothpaste from brushing your teeth or a mint from after lunch. If you can't taste anything, then say your favorite thing to taste.

I had my doubts. I didn't think something so simple could help me, but I decided to try it.

When Monday came, my week was jam-packed with events, school, lessons, and practice. I could feel my anxiety and stress rise.

But then, I remembered there was something I could do about it. I began to look for 5 things to look at, 4 things to touch, 3 sounds to hear, 2 things to smell, and 1 thing to taste.

By the time I got to three things to listen to, I had forgotten what it was I was so stressed about. I finished the 5-4-3-2-1, anyways.

I couldn't believe it. It had worked!

I felt so calm and relaxed. I even did some yoga!

The next day, I had an upcoming test I was studying for. After I was done, I began to feel that familiar feeling of stress rising up within me.

But then, I remembered the 5-4-3-2-1.

And just like the day before, the strategy worked again!

Instead of focusing on things I couldn't control, I focused on the things I could control. And it made all the difference!

Remembering the 5-4-3-2-1 could be your secret weapon against stress.

Visit NinjaLifeHacks.tv for fun, free printables.

@marynhin   @GrowGrit
#NinjaLifeHacks

Mary Nhin   Ninja Life Hacks

Ninja Life Hacks